UNDER THE SEA ANIMALS
SHARKS

Amy Culliford

TABLE OF CONTENTS

Sight Words..2

Words to Know..3

Index..16

A Pelican Book

Teaching Tips for Caregivers and Teachers:
Research shows that one of the best ways for students to learn a new topic is to read about it.

Before Reading
- Read the title and predict what the book will be about.
- Read the "Words to Know" and discuss the meaning of each word.
- Read the back cover to see what the book is about.

During Reading
- When a student gets to a word that is unknown, ask them to look at the rest of the sentence to find clues to help with the meaning of the unknown word.
- Motivate students with praise and encouragement.

After Reading
- Discuss the main idea of the book.
- Ask students to give one detail that they learned in the book.

Sight Words

a	have	of
all	is	out
and	kind	some
are	little	this
big	look	

Words to Know

 fins

 fish

 gills

 shark

 teeth

This is a **shark**.

Sharks are a kind of **fish**.

Some sharks are big, and some sharks are little.

All sharks have **gills**.

All sharks have **fins**.

Look out!
All sharks have **teeth**!

Index

big 8
fish 6, 7
gills 10, 11
little 8

shark 4, 5, 6, 8, 10, 12, 14
teeth 14, 15

Written by: Amy Culliford
Design by: Under the Oaks Media
Series Development: James Earley
Editor: Kim Thompson

Photos: Martin Prochazkacz: cover, p. 13, 15; Kaschibo: p. 4-5; le bouil baptiste: p. 7; Lewis Burnett: p. 9; Zebra0209: p. 11

Library of Congress PCN Data
Sharks / Amy Culliford
Under the Sea Animals
ISBN 978-1-63897-066-8 (hard cover)
ISBN 978-1-63897-152-8 (paperback)
ISBN 978-1-63897-238-9 (EPUB)
ISBN 978-1-63897-324-9 (eBook)
Library of Congress Control Number: 2021945244

Printed in the United States of America.

Seahorse Publishing Company
www.seahorsepub.com

Copyright © 2022 **SEAHORSE PUBLISHING COMPANY**

All rights reserved. No part of this publication may be reproduced, stored in a retrieval system or be transmitted in any form or by any means, electronic, mechanical, photocopying, recording, or otherwise, without the prior written permission of Seahorse Publishing Company.

Published in the United States
Seahorse Publishing
PO Box 771325
Coral Springs, FL 33077